Social Studies for the Creative Mind

Jeffrey B. Harris M.Ed

Dedicated to my students...

Social Studies for the Creative Mind

Jeffrey B. Harris M.Ed

•Yonah Publishing•

Social Studies for the Creative Mind: *Activities That Won't Put Students to Sleep*

By Jeffrey B. Harris

Copyright © April 2013
Alpharetta, Georgia

All rights Reserved. No part of this book may be reproduced or transmitted in any form by any means, electronic or mechanical, including photocopying and recording, or by any information storage and retrieval system, except as may be expressly permitted by the 1976 Copyright Act or in writing from the publisher.

Table of Contents

Introduction
1. Detective   6
2. Dialogue   8
3. Recipe   10
4. Before and After   12
5. Board Game   14
6. Timeline   16
7. Speech   18
8. Skit   20
9. Biography Poster   22
10. Acrostic   24
11. Tagline or slogan   26
12. Letter   28
13. Journal   30
14. Thematic Collage   32
15. Brochure   34
16. Pamphlet   36
17. Advertisements   38
18. Song   40
19. Poem   42
20. Pop-up Book   44
21. Alternative Outcome Story   46
22. Travel through Time   48
23. Crossword Puzzle   50
24. Mock Interview   52
25. Editorial   54
26. Comic Strip   56
27. Political Cartoon   58
28. Story Board   60
29. Propaganda Poster   62
30. Obituary   64
31. Last Will and Testament   66
32. Mental Map   68

Social Studies for the Creative Mind

33.	Speech Clouds	70
34.	Question Cube	72
35.	Real Estate Broker	74
36.	Business Proposal	76
37.	Genre Story	78
38.	Kid's Book	80
39.	Theme Park	82
40.	Memorial	84
41.	Artifact	86
42.	Who Am I?	88
43.	Postcards	90
44.	Newspaper	92
45.	Debate	94
46.	Make Your Own Test	96
47.	Mnemonics	98
48.	Create Class Constitution	100
49.	Paper Fortune Teller	102
50.	Character Project	104
51.	Trading Cards	106
52.	Create a Country	108
53.	Diorama	110
54.	Puppet Show	112
55.	Mobile	114
56.	TV Show	116
57.	News Anchor	118
58.	Create a Review Game	120
59.	Passport	122
60.	Symbolic Map	124
61.	Foldable	126
62.	Creative Journal	128
63.	Wear It!	130

Introduction:

The activities in this book are meant to be manipulated, added to, shuffled, chopped up, mutated, or amended in any way that suits your unit of instruction. These ideas, for the most part, consist of a one-size-fits-all composition. For instance, the 'journal entry' comes across as vague (as it's intended), and the specific criteria and objective is up to you, the teacher. A journal entry allows the student to put themselves in the shoes of someone covered in the curriculum, be it Joseph Stalin, Siddhartha Gautama, a Haitian fisherman, or even a Diet Coke. The content in this book will hopefully be a starting point, or trigger, to your infinite imagination...in lesson creation. In turn, students will not only realize their creative potential, but develop the critical thinking skills they'll use for the rest of their lives.

The time allotted for each activity will vary, as some of the tasks could be used as a warm-up or, just as easily, a week-long project. The times stated are based on the ways in which I've put them to use in the classroom, but can easily be changed to fit any lesson. Each activity's duration is an estimate, not gospel.

Each activity in the pages ahead promotes higher-order thinking skills, but the buck doesn't stop there. Creative thinking is the predominant aim of this book, and for this reason, the specifics for each exercise are broad, leaving room for student innovation. As Joseph Campbell expressed, "the job of an educator is to teach students to see the vitality in themselves."

Challenging multiple intelligences in the classroom involves variety, the other point of this book. People of all levels of intelligence are capable of more than mere rote learning, but each student will do better in some exercises more than others. We, as educators, must provide the variety of canvases, the paint, the brushes, and the enthusiasm, but the students construct, create, and discover.

What's in the book?

There is one page dedicated for each activity, followed by a page for your notes and adjustments. On the activity page the following will be addressed: **Time, materials, arrangement, scenario, procedure, and criteria**. A majority of the exercises will have a basic example(s) for further clarification.

Time, as mentioned before, can and will vary, depending on how you want to use the activity. The **materials** are very basic, and will often only include paper and a writing utensil. The **scenario** sets the stage and acts like a subtitle. The **procedure** lays down the instructions for the exercise. Finally, the **criteria** act as a guide when you form a rubric for each creative task.

People remember more when they are having fun, so do everything you can to make class exciting! I hope you find this book useful and it doesn't end up in your fireplace…

Social Studies for the Creative Mind

The Detective

Time: One Class Period
Materials: Various
Arrangement: Individual or Group

Scenario: Time to solve a mystery and learn at the same time.

Procedure: Have students go on a scavenger hunt for clues to solve a history mystery. Create a handout that explains the day's lesson, but have it be in a question/answer format. The answers will of course be blank. You can put the first clue on the board. For example, Clue One: "you may have to 'swing' to the first answer." The students realize that they have to go to the playground and check out the swings, and there they will find the first answer and the second clue. Make each clue as relevant to the lesson as possible. For example, the previous clue dealing with swings could be about swing music...

Criteria: Content_____
    Factual_____
    Cooperation_____
    Speed_____

Notes

Implementation_____

_____
_____
_____
_____
_____
_____

Changes_____

_____
_____
_____
_____
_____
_____
_____

Results_____

_____
_____
_____
_____
_____
_____
_____

Social Studies for the Creative Mind

Dialogue

Time: 15-20 minutes
Materials: Pencil and Notebook Paper, or Computer
Arrangement: Individual or Group

Scenario: Dialogue involves the discussion between two or more people, usually with the hope of some sort of conflict resolution.

Procedure: Have students take the points of view for famous historical figures, fictional commoners from a specific time period, rivals of belief systems, or even something more abstract, like the belief systems themselves or a lifeless object. They can recite it in front of the class as pairs or groups.

Example: Patent Issues
<u>Thomas Edison</u>: I invented the light bulb!
<u>Joseph Swan</u>: Oh, I beg to differ...
<u>Thomas Edison</u>: Well, at least mine could glow longer, so there...
<u>Joseph Swan</u>: See you in court!

Criteria: Content_____   Comparisons_____
   Factual_____   Original_____

Notes

Implementation _____

_____
_____
_____
_____
_____
_____

Changes _____

_____
_____
_____
_____
_____
_____
_____

Results _____

_____
_____
_____
_____
_____
_____
_____

Recipe

Time: 15-20 Minutes
Materials: Pencil and Notebook Paper, or Computer
Arrangement: Individual or Group

Scenario: A recipe involves the break-down of ingredients and their amounts for a certain meal. It also gives directions involving chronology. Now apply this to a historical event.

Procedure: Have the students choose an event from history; placing all 'ingredients' (causes) and their 'measurements' (significance value) into the theoretical skillet. Then the students should write out the 'instructions' (chronology) for completing the 'meal.' This could also be done as a group activity in which each member of the group chooses to draw one of the 'ingredients'.

Example: <u>The Dish- The American Revolution Casserole</u>

> <u>Ingredients</u>- Two teaspoons of the Sugar Act, a half cup of the Tea Act, one cup of the Declaration of Independence, etc...
> 1. Start by greasing up a casserole dish with a spoon full of French and Indian War, then ...

Criteria: Content_____ Original_____ Causes_____
Factual_____ Evaluate_____

Notes

Implementation_____

_____
_____
_____
_____
_____
_____

Changes_____

_____
_____
_____
_____
_____
_____
_____
_____

Results_____

_____
_____
_____
_____
_____
_____
_____

Before and After

Time: 15-20 Minutes
Materials: Colored Pencils and Notebook Paper, or Computer
Arrangement: Individual

Scenario: This could also be considered a 'cause and effect' activity. This drawing exercise helps explain change.

Procedure: Have students create a T-chart on a piece of paper. At the top of the paper, the students should write down the title of the event. They should draw what it was like before the event on the left side, then the consequence on the right side. If there is something in particular you want to have conveyed, then your instructions must be explicit.

Student Example: <u>Sherman Burning Atlanta</u>

Criteria: Content_____   Original_____
　　　　　　Factual_____   Causes_____

Notes

Implementation_____

Changes_____

Results_____

Board Game

Time: Four 60-Minute Class Periods
Materials: Poster board, Colored Pencils, Scissors (more)
Arrangement: Group

Scenario: Great for a specific region or time period review.

Procedure: The students will create a board game in which the overall objective of the game should revolve around your particular lesson or unit of study. Utilize geography, government, economics, and culture as part of the board itself. Use dice, a spinner, or a question card for each player to advance. Students will create the cards, the board, and the characters; they will then play each other's games for the ultimate review.

Example: <u>Ancient Egypt</u>: A maze in the pyramid. Traverse through secret tunnels, while coming across ancient tombs, mythical creatures, and gods. There is any number of game objectives: escaping the maze with the most amount of treasure or artifacts, rescuing the pharaoh, defeating Anubis, etc.

Criteria: Content_____
         Factual_____
         Original_____
         Aesthetics_____

Notes

Implementation _____

_____
_____
_____
_____
_____

Changes _____

_____
_____
_____
_____
_____
_____
_____

Results _____

_____
_____
_____
_____
_____
_____

Timeline

Time: Varies- 15-60 Minutes
Materials: Pencil and Notebook Paper, or Computer
Arrangement: Individual or Group

Scenario: Timelines show causation, relationships, and the sequence of events. There isn't just one way to do a timeline... What is plotted on a timeline could be anything, from wars to leprechaun sightings. It should be based on a particular theme to avoid haphazard topics with no relevance to one another. Having students illustrate their plots is still another way for their imaginations to run wild.

Procedure: Students should draw a straight line on a piece of paper. Next the students should determine the space between intervals based on the number of events to be placed on the line. Mark the spots on the line and add a description of each event.

Example: <u>Women's Rights</u>

```
Seneca Falls Convention                      Women's Suffrage
1848                                                     1920
|───────────────────────|───────────────────|
                    1890
              Formation of NAWSA
```

Criteria: Content_____   Evaluate_____
            Factual_____
            Original_____

Notes

Implementation _____

_____
_____
_____
_____
_____
_____

Changes _____

_____
_____
_____
_____
_____
_____

Results _____

_____
_____
_____
_____
_____
_____

Speech

Time: Varies- 5 minutes- Several Class Periods
Materials: Pencil and Notebook Paper, Notecards
Arrangement: Individual

Scenario: Speeches are excellent ways for students to demonstrate the mastering of a subject. Starting speeches at a young age is the key for students to overcome the fear of public speaking...

Procedure: Give students a topic on something relevant to your unit of study. They should research the subject and create an outline to start. The next step is to write the speech, followed by the creation of notecards. Finally, PRACTICE. PRACTICE. PRACTICE.

Example: Icebreakers- With a bag filled with pop-culture topics, have the students give a brief, 30 second, impromptu speech. Loads of fun!
Other speech ideas include the following:
    Informative
    Persuasive
    Demonstrative
One more type of speech is 'entertaining.' I find this works best when the students are informed that there should be entertaining elements in all speeches.

Criteria: Content_____   Original_____
            Factual_____   Memorized_____

Notes

Implementation_____

_____
_____
_____
_____
_____
_____

Changes_____

_____
_____
_____
_____
_____
_____
_____

Results_____

_____
_____
_____
_____
_____
_____

Skit

Time: 30-60 minutes
Materials: Pencil, Paper, Notecards
Arrangement: Group

Scenario: Act out a skit involving figures in history- Experiential

Procedure: Have students get in groups of four. Set the criteria so it relates to the unit and requires higher order thinking. They should put themselves in the roles of particular people from history and it should be more elaborate than just a dialogue, perhaps even requiring appropriate attire and props. I like to make situations like this a competition, and the winner gets a prize...

Example: <u>The Civil War:</u>
    Group One: Secession
    Group Two: Confederacy
    Group Three: Union
    Group Four: Day to Day and Technology
    Group Five: The Aftermath

Criteria: Content_____
        Factual_____
        Original_____
        Props_____
        Participation_____

Notes

Implementation_____

_____
_____
_____
_____
_____
_____

Changes_____

_____
_____
_____
_____
_____
_____
_____
_____

Results_____

_____
_____
_____
_____
_____
_____

Social Studies for the Creative Mind

Biography Poster

Time: One - Two Class Periods
Materials: Poster board, scissors, construction paper, tape
Arrangement: Individual

Scenario: Good for a unit of study that covers numerous historical figures; it involves creativity, giving a speech and role play.

Procedure: Students will pick a person of interest and gather relevant facts about said person. They will cut out a hole in the middle of the poster so their face is visible when they hold it up in front of them. They will then design the poster so that it looks as though their person's body is on it. Finally, they should add other things to the poster, like 'thinking clouds' or taglines.

Example: If you have a large class and don't want students using the same people, be sure to do this activity in a lesson that involves numerous people:
Presidents, Wars, Age of Reason, Inventors, or Explorers

Criteria: Content_____
          Factual_____
          Original_____
          Aesthetics_____

Notes

Implementation _____

_____
_____
_____
_____
_____
_____

Changes _____

_____
_____
_____
_____
_____
_____

Results _____

_____
_____
_____
_____
_____
_____

Acrostic

Time: 10-20 Minutes
Materials: Pencil and Notebook Paper, or Computer
Arrangement: Individual

Scenario: A great language arts assignment that truly crosses over to multiple disciplines.

Procedure: Pick a word and write it horizontally. Then, write a word or sentence for each letter in the original word. Obviously, the words or sentences chosen should relate to the word. Furthermore, the words or phrases chosen could also be in chronological sequence for an added challenge.

Example: <u>Union</u>
    USA
    Napoleonic Tactics don't work as well anymore
    Ignite Atlanta, Mr. Sherman
    Onlookers at Bull Run had picnics
    No more slavery!

Criteria: Content_____
         Factual_____
         Original_____
         Elaboration_____

Notes

Implementation _____
_____
_____
_____
_____
_____
_____
_____
_____

Changes _____
_____
_____
_____
_____
_____
_____
_____

Results _____
_____
_____
_____
_____
_____
_____
_____

Tagline or Slogan

Time: 5-15 Minutes
Materials: Pencil and Notebook Paper, or Computer
Arrangement: Individual or Group

Scenario: Create a short, catchy phrase describing a person, product, or an event. This is a perfect time to bring in some language arts and utilize alliteration.

Procedure: Students should come up with catch phrases. This works best for products or inventions. This would be a great activity if you're covering turn-of-the-century inventions.

Example: Terminator- "I'll be back"
Skittles- "Taste the Rainbow"
Timex- "Takes a licking and keeps on ticking"

Criteria: Relevance_____
Factual_____
Original_____

Notes

Implementation _____

_____
_____
_____
_____
_____
_____

Changes _____

_____
_____
_____
_____
_____
_____

Results _____

_____
_____
_____
_____
_____
_____

Letter

Time: 15-25 Minutes
Materials: Pencil and Notebook Paper, or Computer
Arrangement: Individual

Scenario: Point of view of the common person, elite, gender, child or even animal during a certain time period.

Procedure: Writing a letter allows a student to not only wear the shoes of someone from the past, but someone with a different way of life. Students can write a letter that fits in the categories of speeches: informative, persuasive, and demonstrative, but could also be a farewell. Have students include facts and criticism about a particular idea of the time or region within the unit of study.

Example: A letter home from George Washington during Valley Forge

Criteria: Content_____
Factual_____
Original_____
Understanding_____

Notes

Implementation _____

_____
_____
_____
_____
_____
_____

Changes _____

_____
_____
_____
_____
_____
_____

Results _____

_____
_____
_____
_____
_____
_____

Social Studies for the Creative Mind

Journal

Time: 15-30 Minutes
Materials: Pencil and Notebook Paper, or Computer
Arrangement: Individual

Scenario: Another point of view activity.

Procedure: The journal entry can allow the student to, not only where the shoes of someone else, but delve deep into the emotions that are prevalent, given the circumstances of the situation.

Examples: Daily entries of a child laborer, astronaut, soldier in Genghis Khan's army, a monk in the middle ages, a war horse from WWI, or a mouse living in a field hospital during the Civil War.

Criteria: Content_____
          Factual_____
          Original_____

Notes

Implementation _____
_____
_____
_____
_____
_____
_____
_____

Changes _____
_____
_____
_____
_____
_____
_____
_____

Results _____
_____
_____
_____
_____
_____
_____

Thematic Collage

Time: 30-120 Minutes
Materials: Paper, Colored Pencils, Glue, Scissors (magazines)
Arrangement: Individual or Group

Scenario: A great review activity and a way for students to collaborate and categorize information.

Procedure: Using magazines, the internet, or just their imaginations, students will cut out, print, or create images and paste them onto a poster board. I enjoy putting the class into multiple groups and setting a time limit. This can be done in a competition style and the criteria should be based on content, aesthetics, and quantity of images.

Example: Innovations of the early Latin American Civilizations

Criteria: Content_____
  Factual_____
  Original_____
  Aesthetics_____
  Quantity_____

Notes

Implementation_____

_____
_____
_____
_____
_____
_____

Changes_____

_____
_____
_____
_____
_____
_____
_____
_____

Results_____

_____
_____
_____
_____
_____
_____
_____

Brochure

Time: 30-60 Minutes
Materials: Colored Pencils and Paper, or Computer (Software)
Arrangement: Individual or Group

Scenario: An extensive ad for a certain country or region... This helps discover geographical and historical themes like culture, economics, politics, and geography.

Procedure: This could be created on different types of software, but it can just as easily be done with good old fashioned paper and colored pencils. The students should be given a country and the objective is to make the country as appealing as possible. This is a great opportunity to explain bias and propaganda. Set the criteria to include more than just the tourist charm, but economics and politics as well. Give each student a piece of computer paper and have them create a trifold.

Example: Overall theme: 'Come to Cuba, our people suffer, but you won't!'

Criteria: Content_____
Factual_____
Original_____
Aesthetics_____

Notes

Implementation _____

_____
_____
_____
_____
_____
_____

Changes _____

_____
_____
_____
_____
_____
_____

Results _____

_____
_____
_____
_____
_____
_____

Pamphlet

Time: 30-60 Minutes
Materials: Colored Pencils, Paper, Computer (software)
Arrangement: Individual or Group

Scenario: An advertisement for a cause... using opinions and bias

Procedure: Similar to a brochure, but this is for a particular cause or belief. Students can familiarize themselves with opinion writing while covering a certain topic.

Example: Greek Mythology (Follow Apollo), Join the Chinese Communist Revolution, Join the Anti-Federalists, Prepare for Nuclear War!, or Learn how to meditate and follow the Buddha way, today!

Criteria: Content_____
  Factual_____
  Original_____
  Aesthetics_____

Notes

Implementation_____

_____
_____
_____
_____
_____
_____

Changes_____

_____
_____
_____
_____
_____
_____
_____

Results_____

_____
_____
_____
_____
_____
_____
_____

Advertisements

Time: 5-15 Minutes
Materials: Colored Pencils and Paper
Arrangement: Individual or Group

Scenario: Create advertisements for period technology, businesses, food, etc.

Procedure: This exercise can be by itself or part of something larger, like a newspaper or brochure. It can be used to cover the material possessions of a time period or to explain inflation.

Example: An advertisement from 1892 for bicycles- $5.00

Criteria: Content_____
Factual_____
Original_____
Aesthetics_____

Notes

Implementation _____

_____
_____
_____
_____
_____
_____

Changes _____

_____
_____
_____
_____
_____
_____
_____
_____

Results _____

_____
_____
_____
_____
_____
_____
_____

Song

Time: 15-25 Minutes
Materials: Pencil and Notebook Paper, or Computer
Arrangement: Individual or Group

Scenario: Create a song about the lesson.

Procedure: This is a great activity for pairs of students. They can change the lyrics to a preexisting song or start from scratch. Set the criteria so that a certain number of facts from the unit are put into the song. This can be very entertaining if they sing or rap in front of the class. Of course that should probably be voluntary; considering public speaking is feared more than death...public singing might just CAUSE death...

Example: Think of something with a catchy rhythm and a repeating chorus

Criteria: Content_____
   Factual_____
   Original_____
   Length_____

Notes

Implementation _____

_____
_____
_____
_____
_____

Changes _____

_____
_____
_____
_____
_____

Results _____

_____
_____
_____
_____
_____

Poem

Time: 15-30 Minutes
Materials: Pencil and Notebook Paper, or Computer
Arrangement: Individual or Group

Scenario: Rhyme about something from the lesson.

Procedure: Although poems don't have to contain rhymes, it's a lot more fun when the students try it. When a student says, "nothing rhymes with orange" and they just have to have that word, then tell them to use it at the beginning of the line, not the end...

Example: Student's Civil War Poem

Traveler was the pride of Robert E. Lee
Thomas Jackson was a stonewall and wouldn't flee
Nathan Forrest was controversial to say the least
William Sherman had the heart of a beast

Criteria: Content_____
          Factual_____
          Original_____
          Rhyme_____

Notes

Implementation _____

_____
_____
_____
_____
_____
_____

Changes _____

_____
_____
_____
_____
_____
_____

Results _____

_____
_____
_____
_____
_____
_____

Pop-Up Book

Time: 20-30 Minutes
Materials: Colored Pencils Paper, Scissors, Glue
Arrangement: Group

Scenario: Great review book with figures, buildings, technology- make it a competition.

Procedure: This exercise is great for groups in which everyone makes a page. Students can use one sheet of paper of the background and another to cut up and manipulate. Tell the students to be careful with glue; it could cause the pages to stick together...

Example: Inventions, presidents, laws, customs, etc.

Criteria: Content_____
Factual_____
Original_____
Aesthetics_____

Notes

Implementation_____

_____
_____
_____
_____
_____
_____
_____

Changes_____

_____
_____
_____
_____
_____
_____
_____

Results_____

_____
_____
_____
_____
_____
_____

Social Studies for the Creative Mind

Alternative Outcome Story

Time: 25-45 Minutes
Materials: Pencil and Notebook Paper, or Computer
Arrangement: Individual

Scenario: Take an event in history and change it; what does the future hold?

Procedure: This activity helps students understand causation. Pick a situation from the past and either pretend it didn't happen or something else happened in its place. Then have students create a different present day.

Example: The bombing of Pearl Harbor never happened, We lost WWII, JFK wasn't assassinated, The South won the Civil War, or the automobile was invented 50 years earlier.

Criteria: Content_____
         Factual_____
         Original_____
         Understanding_____

Notes

Implementation _____

_____
_____
_____
_____
_____
_____

Changes _____

_____
_____
_____
_____
_____
_____

Results _____

_____
_____
_____
_____
_____
_____

Travel through Time

Time: 25-45 Minutes
Materials: Pencil and Notebook Paper, or Computer
Arrangement: Individual

Scenario: Add a little science fiction to your lesson and view, change, or stop famous events.

Procedure: You travel back in time and change a certain event. Come back in time and discuss how life is different. This can also be done with travel to the future explaining causes of future concepts. Have students create a story mixing fiction and facts.

Example: Travel 150 years into the future... There's no more advanced technology. What caused this to happen? WWIII... Welcome back to the Stone Age!

Criteria: Content_____
Factual_____
Original_____
Elaboration_____

Notes

Implementation _____

_____
_____
_____
_____
_____

Changes _____

_____
_____
_____
_____
_____

Results _____

_____
_____
_____
_____
_____

Crossword Puzzle

Time: 20-30 Minutes
Materials: Pencil and Notebook Paper, or Computer (software)
Arrangement: Individual

Scenario: Use a puzzle maker online or just do it by hand. It puts a great spin on learning new vocabulary.

Procedure: This can help students learn new vocabulary or concepts from the unit AND help them with spelling. Have the students use graph paper and create questions for 'down' and 'across'.

Example:

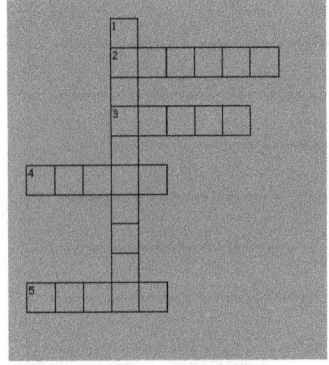

Across
2. God of Music
3. Congressmen in favor of war
4. General for the Union
5. This river is located in China

Down.
1. First President of the U.S

Criteria: Content_____
Factual_____
Original_____
Number_____

Notes

Implementation _____

_____
_____
_____
_____
_____
_____
_____

Changes _____

_____
_____
_____
_____
_____
_____
_____
_____
_____

Results _____

_____
_____
_____
_____
_____
_____

Mock Interview

Time: 20-40 Minutes
Materials: Pencil and Notebook Paper, Notecards
Arrangement: Group of Individual

Scenario: Interview characters from history. Similar to a dialogue...

Procedure: Students should conduct a fake interview with a person from the unit of study or a made-up person that can relate to the lesson. This can be in a question/answer format, with questions that may enlighten the audience with information that goes beyond the textbook. For added fun, it could be done in front of the class, not just on paper.

Example: An interview with Poseidon

Jimmy: So where do you like to hang out when you're not working?
Poseidon: Uh, the ocean, duh...
Jimmy: How's your relationship with your father?
Poseidon: Considering that he swallowed me, not that great.
Jimmy: Do you have any children?
Poseidon: Ever heard of Pegasus, the flying horse...?

Criteria: Content_____
  Factual_____
  Original_____

Notes

Implementation _____
_____
_____
_____
_____
_____
_____

Changes _____
_____
_____
_____
_____
_____
_____
_____

Results _____
_____
_____
_____
_____
_____
_____

Editorial

Time: 15-25 Minutes
Materials: Pencil and Notebook Paper, or Computer
Arrangement: Individual

Scenario: Opinion articles from your view or that of a historical figure dealing with an important event.

Procedure: Pick a controversial event relating to your current unit of study and cover both sides of the issue with as little bias as possible. Have the students pick a side or you can do it for them. They should write about a page that is completely one-sided.

Example: Chester Arthur was the best president and here's why: 1. His beard was unique. 2. He did the best he could after being forced into office following the death of Garfield...the president, not the cat.

Criteria: Relevance_____
             Factual_____
             Original_____

Notes

Implementation_____

_____
_____
_____
_____
_____
_____
_____

Changes_____

_____
_____
_____
_____
_____
_____
_____

Results_____

_____
_____
_____
_____
_____
_____
_____

Comic Strip

Time: 10-15 Minutes
Materials: Colored Pencils, Paper
Arrangement: Individual

Scenario: Use some humor or just tell the facts. Create a comic involving the day's lesson.

Procedure: Show your students some examples from the funny pages in the paper. Be sure the students know that it has to revolve around the unit and see what they come up with. They will certainly surprise you with their wit and their punch lines.

Criteria: Content_____
   Factual_____
   Original_____
   Aesthetics_____

Notes

Implementation _____

_____
_____
_____
_____
_____
_____

Changes _____

_____
_____
_____
_____
_____
_____

Results _____

_____
_____
_____
_____
_____
_____

Political Cartoon

Time: 10-15 Minutes
Materials: Colored Pencils, Paper
Arrangement: Individual

Scenario: Sum up a historical event in a drawing using symbolism.

Procedure: To make sure the students don't just make a drawing, examples will be needed. Political or editorial cartoons involve symbolism and make a clear point. For example, if one were to draw a political cartoon about how one politician behaved extremely aggressive during a debate, the student could ask, 'what else acts aggressively'? On the other side of the coin, the student could think of the other politician as weak or timid. The cartoon could depict a debate between a bear and a mouse, using symbolism to drive the point home.

Criteria: Content_____
Factual_____
Original_____
Symbolism_____

Notes

Implementation _____

_____
_____
_____
_____
_____
_____

Changes _____

_____
_____
_____
_____
_____
_____
_____
_____

Results _____

_____
_____
_____
_____
_____
_____

Story Board

Time: 15-30 Minutes
Materials: Pencils, Paper
Arrangement: Individual

Scenario: A graphic depiction of events in an episode using 6-8 illustrations.

Procedure: This could be seen as a hybrid of a comic strip and a timeline. It can also explain causation, if done the right way, and helps prioritize the information from a particular lesson. If you set the limit of illustrations to six, it will force the students to decide between multitudes of concepts and pick what they deem the most important. You could also have the students write out on a separate sheet of paper why they chose the events in their story board.

Examples: Turning points in wars, the feminist movement, the migration and assimilation of people to the U.S., the decolonization of Africa, or the civil rights movement

Criteria: Content_____
Factual_____
Original_____
Sequence_____

Notes

Implementation _____
_____
_____
_____
_____
_____
_____

Changes _____
_____
_____
_____
_____
_____
_____

Results _____
_____
_____
_____
_____
_____
_____

Propaganda Poster

Time: 25-40 Minutes
Materials: Pencil and Notebook Paper, Poster board
Arrangement: Individual

Scenario: Show some from WWI or II and have them create their own.

Procedure: After your students have a working understanding of the meaning of propaganda, they can create their own. Just as a persuasive essay is trying to sway the reader in a definite direction, propaganda aims to influence an audience using absolute bias, or one side of an argument. If you see a poster of two people fighting, one with angelic features and a shirt that says 'USA', while the other person is somewhat demonic, with a shirt that says 'USSR', who will you root for?

Example: Uncle Sam and posters for buying war bonds

Criteria: Content_____
Factual_____
Original_____
Bias_____

Notes

Implementation _____

_____
_____
_____
_____
_____
_____
_____

Changes _____

_____
_____
_____
_____
_____
_____
_____
_____
_____
_____

Results _____

_____
_____
_____
_____
_____
_____

Obituary

Time: 10-15 Minutes
Materials: Pencil and Notebook Paper, or Computer
Arrangement: Individual

Scenario: Prioritizing information and point of view.

Procedure: Once you get past the morbidity this can be a fun activity. (Yeah, that rhymed) This is a great way to have students prioritize information about a person from the unit, putting a positive spin (or negative) on their achievements in life.

Example: There are archives of obituaries for some famous Americans at earlyamerica.com.

Criteria: Content_____
Factual_____
Original_____
Evaluation_____

Notes

Implementation _____

_____
_____
_____
_____
_____
_____

Changes _____

_____
_____
_____
_____
_____
_____

Results _____

_____
_____
_____
_____
_____
_____

Last Will and Testament

Time: 30-40 Minutes
Materials: Pencil and Notebook Paper, or Computer
Arrangement: Individual

Scenario: Another somewhat morbid activity that deals with point of view.

Procedure: Students can delve into the time period of the unit and focus on what a particular person may have deemed important. Students can study technology and innovations of the time period and leave certain important possessions to loved ones, while even leaving other possessions of significant metaphorical meaning to enemies.

Example: JFK's Will
Golf Clubs to his brother, Robert.
The cat's dirty litter box to Fidel Castro.

Criteria: Content_____
　　　　　　Factual_____
　　　　　　Original_____

Notes

Implementation _____

_____
_____
_____
_____
_____
_____
_____

Changes _____

_____
_____
_____
_____
_____
_____
_____
_____

Results _____

_____
_____
_____
_____
_____
_____

Mental Map

Time: 10-30 Minutes
Materials: Pencil and Notebook Paper
Arrangement: Individual

Scenario: Have students create a map of a region before it is covered, then again after the geography unit is covered or before the map test.

Procedure: A great assessment exercise to see what your students already know about the geography of a certain region. The students should create a map of a region from scratch, with no help from a reference map. You can also have them create a map of their town, which will help with some of the themes of geography.

Criteria: Content_____
         Factual_____
         Original_____
         Elaboration_____

Notes

Implementation _____

_____
_____
_____
_____
_____

Changes _____

_____
_____
_____
_____
_____

Results _____

_____
_____
_____
_____
_____

Speech Clouds

Time: 15-20 Minutes
Materials: Pencil, Paper
Arrangement: Individual or Group

Scenario: A perfect review activity that allows the students to review their knowledge of specific people from the unit.

Procedure: Using projected primary photos of historical figures, have students create thought/speech bubbles on the whiteboard depicting their point of view. A fun way to do this is to show the students a photo of someone like George Washington. Then give them a moment to jot down two speech or thought bubbles. One should be content driven, showing that they know important details about Washington. The other bubble should be humorous, but still deal with the content. Have them turn in the sheets and you can make the bubbles on the board for the top three in each category.

Criteria: Content_____
Factual_____
Original_____
Participation_____

Notes

Implementation _____

_____
_____
_____
_____
_____
_____

Changes _____

_____
_____
_____
_____
_____
_____

Results _____

_____
_____
_____
_____
_____
_____

Question Cube Game

Time: 20-45 Minutes
Materials: Paper, Pencil, Scissors, Tape or Glue
Arrangement: Individual or Group

Scenario: Create a paper cube with concepts from the unit on each side, get with a partner, and roll each other's cube three times.

Procedure: Each individual creates one; putting vocabulary, questions, or pictures on each side then gets in pairs to roll and give the answer - Keep score. Each round should consist of three rolls per student. After thirty rolls, stop the game and add up the points. The top three students get a prize.

Criteria: Content_____
Factual_____
Original_____
Participation_____

Notes

Implementation _____

_____
_____
_____
_____
_____
_____

Changes _____

_____
_____
_____
_____
_____
_____

Results _____

_____
_____
_____
_____
_____
_____

Real Estate Broker

Time: 20-30 Minutes
Materials: Pencil, Paper
Arrangement: Individual or Group

Scenario: Cover architecture and period technology by acting as a realtor.

Procedure: This activity works great for an ancient civilizations unit. Students can put a price or value on buildings like the Parthenon, the Pyramids of Giza, the Taj Mahal, etc... Then they can write brief selling points for potential buyers. They should include a number of facts about the structure and the area, but should also be persuasive in their synopsis.

Example: The Sphinx of Giza
 Title: 'A handyman's dream"
 Price: $1,000,000
 Built: 2500 BC by Pharaoh Khafra
 Worship the Sun the right way with the largest monolithic structure in the world!

Criteria: Content_____
 Factual_____
 Original_____
 Aesthetics_____

Notes

Implementation _____

_____
_____
_____
_____
_____
_____

Changes _____

_____
_____
_____
_____
_____
_____
_____

Results _____

_____
_____
_____
_____
_____
_____

Business Proposal

Time: 10-25 Minutes
Materials: Pencil, Paper
Arrangement: Individual or Group

Scenario: Come up with a fictional business plan for a company in a country based on their resources.

Procedure: Depending on the unit being covered, this activity will place your students in the shoes of a salesman and create a business plan based on the resources available for their chosen country.

Example: Honduras- Bananas: Why they have the best and why you <another country> should by them.

Criteria: Content_____
　　　　　　Factual_____
　　　　　　Original_____

Notes

Implementation _____

_____
_____
_____
_____
_____
_____

Changes _____

_____
_____
_____
_____
_____
_____

Results _____

_____
_____
_____
_____
_____
_____

Social Studies for the Creative Mind

Genre Story

Time: 30-45 Minutes
Materials: Pencil and Notebook Paper, or Computer
Arrangement: Group

Scenario: Dividing class into genres and creating a fictional story about the same character, using knowledge from the unit.

Procedure: Put the class into groups of three and assign each group a specific genre, like 'action-adventure', 'romance', 'sci-fi', 'comedy', etc. Each group should write a story revolving around the same character. You must set some ground rules so that each group's story will continue from the previous group. You must designate one group for the beginning and one group for the end and make sure that no group in between 'kills off' the main character or puts him in a situation that prevents continuity. Each group must add a specific number of facts that deal with the unit or lesson. This assignment involves lots of laughs.

Criteria: Content_____
  Factual_____
  Original_____
  Elaboration_____

Notes

Implementation_____

_____
_____
_____
_____
_____
_____

Changes_____

_____
_____
_____
_____
_____
_____
_____

Results_____

_____
_____
_____
_____
_____
_____

Kid's Book

Time: 30-120 Minutes
Materials: Colored Pencils, Paper, (Scissors, Tape)
Arrangement: Group

Scenario: Create your own children's book based on a topic in history or geography.

Procedure: Each student in class can create a page of a children's book and then you can put it together. It works best if it flows like a storyboard, but the theme could be as broad as U.S. history. It's important that the students understand that they are writing for much younger students, and the material should easily be understood. It would be best if all the pages were titled and included a simple drawing. You can give this to the school's librarian to read to younger students, or set up a time for a couple of students to go to the younger grades and read it aloud to the class.

Criteria: Content_____
         Factual_____
         Original_____
         Aesthetics_____

Notes

Implementation _____
_____
_____
_____
_____
_____
_____

Changes _____
_____
_____
_____
_____
_____
_____

Results _____
_____
_____
_____
_____
_____
_____

Theme Park

Time: 2 - 3 Class Periods
Materials: Poster board, Colored Pencils, Tape, Glue (more)
Arrangement: Group

Scenario: Create a park that includes all the attributes of the culture, time period, or region you are covering.

Procedure: Place students in small groups and have them come up with a theme park. For example, if the theme park was based on Ancient Egypt, the students could have souvenir shops that sell pharaoh dolls, Anubis t-shirts, or honey and date ice cream. Also, they could create rides like 'Raft the Nile' or the 'Pyramid Rollercoaster'. Set up a number of facts that must be presented in their project and just wait to see what they come up with!

Criteria: Content_____
   Factual_____
   Original_____
   Aesthetics_____

Notes

Implementation _____

_____
_____
_____
_____
_____
_____

Changes _____

_____
_____
_____
_____
_____
_____

Results _____

_____
_____
_____
_____
_____
_____

Memorial

Time: 15-45 Minutes
Materials: Paper, Pencil or Modeling Clay
Arrangement: Individual or Group

Scenario: Create your own statue that represents a specific theme in history.

Procedure: Have students research a famous figure from the unit. They will then create a memorial to that person that fits with their achievements. The students will use clay to mold a representation of something significant in a historical figure's life.

Example: Zachary Taylor- A pick axe- representing the gold rush

Criteria: Content_____
  Factual_____
  Original_____
  Aesthetics_____

Notes

Implementation _____

_____
_____
_____
_____
_____
_____

Changes _____

_____
_____
_____
_____
_____
_____

Results _____

_____
_____
_____
_____
_____
_____

Artifact

Time: 10-60 Minutes
Materials: Paper, Pencil, or Modeling Clay
Arrangement: Individual or Group

Scenario: Using clay to mold an artifact- Prioritizing information...

Procedure: After thoroughly covering a unit or lesson, have each student come up with, and create with clay, an artifact that best represents the time period or culture being covered. Have each student submit in writing the artifact they chose and why it represents the most important concept from the unit.

Example: A Unit on the Civil War
A camera, a railroad car, or the telegraph

Criteria: Content_____
Factual_____
Original_____

Notes

Implementation _____

_____
_____
_____
_____
_____
_____
_____

Changes _____

_____
_____
_____
_____
_____
_____
_____

Results _____

_____
_____
_____
_____
_____
_____
_____

Who am I?

Time: 10-25 Minutes
Materials: Pencil, Paper
Arrangement: Individual or group

Scenario: Having students ask questions to deduce who they are...

Procedure: This can be done in a number of ways. One way would involve creating flash cards with a significant person on it. Hand them out face down, so they don't know who their person is. Then they can tape it to their forehead (or their back so to avoid injury). Lastly, they can get with a partner and ask only five questions to figure out the mystery.

Another way would be to have each student pick a person and write down five facts about the person, with the first facts being the most difficult. They can come up to the front of the class and say one fact at a time, while calling on three students (at the most) per fact, until someone gets it right.

Criteria: Content_____
          Factual_____
          Original_____

Notes

Implementation _____

_____
_____
_____
_____
_____
_____

Changes _____

_____
_____
_____
_____
_____
_____

Results _____

_____
_____
_____
_____
_____

Postcards

Time: 10-20 Minutes
Materials: Notecards, Colored Pencils
Arrangement: Individual

Scenario: Writing to a friend and sharing some geography.

Procedure: Hand out flash cards to your students. On one side they will need to draw a picture depicting something of importance from your unit. On the other side, they will write to a friend describing where they've been and include a few facts to help reinforce the lesson. They will then place them in a bag in the front of the classroom. You should then have each student reach into the bag and receive a postcard to read to the class.

Criteria: Content_____
          Factual_____
          Original_____
          Aesthetics_____

Notes

Implementation _____

_____
_____
_____
_____
_____
_____

Changes _____

_____
_____
_____
_____
_____
_____
_____

Results _____

_____
_____
_____
_____
_____
_____
_____

Newspaper

Time: One – Two Class Periods
Materials: Paper (big), Scissors, Glue, Colored Pencils
Arrangement: Group

Scenario: This involves all the aspects of newspaper: editorial, sports section, current event article, weather, crossword, comics, ads, classifieds, word jumble, etc... or just an individual newspaper's front page.

Procedure: This is a great review assignment that involves teamwork and competition. Divide the class in half. Write the different aspects of a newspaper on the board (ads, headline news story, comics, weather, editorial, etc). They will need to check off every category. Have each group vote on an 'Editor in Chief'. They will assign each member a specific duty and oversee the entire process. Give each group a poster board or large sheet of paper; 24'x36' works best. Give them a class period or two and grade them on the number of facts, aesthetics, and originality.

Criteria: Content_____
Factual_____
Original_____
Aesthetics_____

Notes

Implementation_____

_____
_____
_____
_____
_____
_____

Changes_____

_____
_____
_____
_____
_____
_____
_____

Results_____

_____
_____
_____
_____
_____
_____

Debate

Time: Two Class Periods - 5 Class Periods
Materials: Pencil, Paper, Notecards
Arrangement: Group

Scenario: Active learning that deepens thinking skills.

Procedure: Put students in groups of two going head to head against another group. Have each group give introductions to their sides, followed by two sets of rebuttals. Then the groups will field questions from the rest of the class and end with a concluding statement from both teams. Have the rest of the class vote on the winner.

Examples: Capital Punishment, Drug Legalization, Global Warming, Freedom of Speech, Popular Sovereignty

Criteria: Content_____
          Factual_____
          Original_____
          Participation_____

Notes

Implementation _____

Changes _____

Results _____

Make your own Test

Time: 30-60 Minutes
Materials: Paper, Pencil
Arrangement: Individual or Group

Scenario: Do you know how to get students excited about taking a test? Let them make it themselves...

Procedure: It's important that the students have boundaries during this assignment. Otherwise, they will make it either too easy or too difficult. It's also important that they create an answer key on a separate sheet of paper, as well. Have the students pick from a variety of assessment styles, like multiple choice, essay, short answer, fill in the blank, or true/false. Set the number of questions to around 15 to 20, so they can finish in a reasonable amount of time.

Criteria: Content_____
  Factual_____
  Original_____
  Elaboration_____

Notes

Implementation _____

_____
_____
_____
_____
_____

Changes _____

_____
_____
_____
_____
_____

Results _____

_____
_____
_____
_____
_____

Mnemonics

Time: 20-30 Minutes
Materials: Paper, Pencil
Arrangement: Individual or Group

Scenario: Great technique for all learning styles to help remember anything!

Procedure: Whether your student is in medical school or is a fifteen year old on a fifth grade learning level, mnemonic strategies work. Mnemonics involve word association. When going over certain vocabulary words, it may be best to associate the word with something the student already knows. Letter association is the one we're all the most familiar with... Remember 'please excuse my dear aunt sally' to help with the order of operations in math class? P- Parentheses, E- Exponents, M- Multiply, etc. They can be as short as memorizing the Great Lakes or as long as memorizing all the state capitals.

Example: poems, acronyms, easy word phrases
    HOMES = the Great Lakes

Criteria: Content_____
    Factual_____
    Original_____

Notes

Implementation _____

_____
_____
_____
_____
_____

Changes _____

_____
_____
_____
_____
_____

Results _____

_____
_____
_____
_____

Create Class Constitution

Time: 20-45 Minutes
Materials: Paper, Pencil
Arrangement: Individual or Group

Scenario: Time to learn about the government!

Procedure: This is the perfect activity before going over the U.S. Constitution,
In the beginning of the year, have students create the functions of the classroom, followed by a student bill of rights. You'll be surprised at what they will come up with. Guide them, but don't tell them explicitly what to do. The key is for them to understand that they need freedom, not chaos, and structure, not a dictatorship.
Example:

Criteria: Content_____
           Factual_____
           Original_____
           Participation_____

Notes

Implementation _____

_____
_____
_____
_____
_____
_____
_____

Changes _____

_____
_____
_____
_____
_____
_____
_____

Results _____

_____
_____
_____
_____
_____
_____
_____

Paper Fortune Teller

Time: 45-60 Minutes
Materials: Paper, Colored Pencils (markers), Scissors
Arrangement: Individual

Scenario: Pick a color...

Procedure: Pick a theme that's relevant to your unit and have students create paper fortune tellers. (If you don't know how to make one, enlist a student who does to demonstrate how to make them). There are instructions all over the internet on how to make them.
You must start with a square sheet, and then fold each point or corner in, to the center of the square. Now you have a smaller square. Flip it over and repeat the previous steps (fold corners to the center). Unfold to write questions and answers. You can have up to 8 questions in each fortune teller and the students will love using them as a review tool.

Criteria: Content_____
           Factual_____
           Original_____

Notes

Implementation _____

_____
_____
_____
_____
_____
_____
_____

Changes _____

_____
_____
_____
_____
_____
_____
_____

Results _____

_____
_____
_____
_____
_____
_____
_____

Character Project

Time: One Class Period or Two Weeks
Materials: Various
Arrangement: Individual

Scenario: Create character, with personal documents- journal, birth and death certificates, news article, a will, licenses, awards, picture, letters, biography, and an obituary.

Procedure: I usually do this activity during the unit that covers the Civil War. Students will create numerous documents, like the ones mentioned above, dealing with a character they made up. For the Civil War, the character could be a general, deserter, nurse, slave, or spy. This project could be done using templates found on the internet or by hand. Students can turn it all in using a manila envelope or something more creative if they'd like. You must set the content criteria so they will include facts from the unit.

Criteria: Content_____
  Factual_____
  Original_____
  Aesthetics_____

Notes

Implementation_____

_____
_____
_____
_____
_____
_____

Changes_____

_____
_____
_____
_____
_____
_____

Results_____

_____
_____
_____
_____
_____
_____

Trading Cards

Time: 15-45 Minutes
Materials: Notecards, Colored Pencils
Arrangement: Individual or Group

Scenario: Just like baseball cards, Garbage Pail Kids, or Pokémon cards.

Procedure: Students will have a blast creating cards for people being covered in the unit or made up characters with traits of the region or culture in the lesson. On the front of a flash card the students should draw their specific person and have their 'stats' on the back. The information on the back could be accomplishments, life events, or fun facts

Criteria: Organization_____
          Content_____
          Factual_____
          Original_____

Notes

Implementation _____

_____
_____
_____
_____
_____
_____

Changes _____

_____
_____
_____
_____
_____
_____
_____
_____

Results _____

_____
_____
_____
_____
_____
_____
_____

Create a Country

Time: One-Several Class Periods
Materials: Paper and Pencil
Arrangement: Individual or Group

Scenario: Pretend you purchased an Island and you can make it any way you want...

Procedure: Your students can create a country from one that already exists or a deserted island. It's up to the students to figure out how it should be run. What sort of economy will it have? Government? Geography? Energy? Resources? Military? And so on...

Example: <u>Freedomville</u>
    Free Market Economy
    A Federal Republic
    Two Year mandatory military service
    ETC...

Criteria: Content_____
         Factual_____
         Original_____
         Understanding_____

Notes

Implementation_____

_____
_____
_____
_____
_____
_____

Changes_____

_____
_____
_____
_____
_____
_____

Results_____

_____
_____
_____
_____
_____
_____

Diorama

Time: Two Class Periods
Materials: Shoebox, Scissors, Glue, Paper, Colored Pencils (more)
Arrangement: Individual or Group

Scenario: The shoebox scene

Procedure: Students can show a scene from the unit in a shoebox. Some things to consider are scale, background, and materials. It doesn't necessarily have to be in a shoebox, any sort of box will do.

Criteria: Content_____
       Factual_____
       Original_____
       Aesthetics_____

Notes

Implementation _____

_____
_____
_____
_____
_____
_____

Changes _____

_____
_____
_____
_____
_____
_____

Results _____

_____
_____
_____
_____
_____
_____

Puppet Show

Time: One - Two Class Periods
Materials: Various (sock, markers)
Arrangement: Individual or Group

Scenario: Have a skit or dialogue with the historical figures as puppets.

Procedure: Students should bring in some socks and any other materials that can be used as clothes or hair. The puppets can be any person relevant to the lesson you're teaching. When it comes down to show time, it is best to flip over a table for the puppeteers to hide behind. Make sure they write down their dialogue and have a copy for each puppeteer.

Criteria: Content_____
          Factual_____
          Original_____

Notes

Implementation_____

_____
_____
_____
_____
_____

Changes_____

_____
_____
_____
_____
_____

Results_____

_____
_____
_____
_____
_____

Mobile

Time: 60 Minutes
Materials: String, Paper, Colored Pencils, Hangers (more)
Arrangement: Individual or Group

Scenario: Decorate your room with your student's hanging imagination.

Procedure: Using two wire hangers, students should have them cross each other and twist the top so that the curved parts are parallel. Attach all sorts of decorative items with string (obviously you will set the criteria).

Example: The people involved during the Age of Exploration

Criteria: Content_____
          Factual_____
          Original_____
          Aesthetics_____

Notes

Implementation _____

_____
_____
_____
_____
_____
_____

Changes _____

_____
_____
_____
_____
_____
_____

Results _____

_____
_____
_____
_____
_____
_____

Social Studies for the Creative Mind

TV Show

Time: Several Class Periods
Materials: Various
Arrangement: Group

Scenario: Creating a pilot for a major network based on a relevant scenario from your unit of study.

Procedure: Have students use their wild imaginations to create a drama, action, sci-fi, or situation comedy series that takes place during the same time as the lesson you're covering. This could be set up as a skit or be recorded. Some students can help with props and the set, while others can be the actors. It could also be done as an individual activity where each student comes up with a pilot outline and you don't have to get to the point of performing a skit.

Example: *Seinfeld* in 15th Century China

Criteria: Content_____
          Factual_____
          Original_____

Notes

Implementation_____

_____
_____
_____
_____
_____
_____

Changes_____

_____
_____
_____
_____
_____
_____

Results_____

_____
_____
_____
_____
_____
_____

News Anchor

Time: Several Class Periods
Materials: Various
Arrangement: Individual or Group

Scenario: Students can record a news show or just act it out as a skit...either way; they get to talk in that news reporter voice!

Procedure: Show part of a local news program so students have an idea of how it all works. Afterwards, they can choose a time period or region and make sure the news stories are relevant. Have students work in groups of four and be sure to include two anchors, a sports anchor, and maybe even a meteorologist to show geography. This is a great activity to be recorded.

Example: News Anchor of the Renaissance or Modern Day Mongolia

Criteria: Content_____
          Factual_____
          Original_____
          Organization_____

Notes

Implementation _____

_____
_____
_____
_____
_____

Changes _____

_____
_____
_____
_____
_____

Results _____

_____
_____
_____
_____
_____

Create a Review Game

Time: 15-20 minutes
Materials: Various
Arrangement: Individual or Group

Scenario: Put the students mind to work and have them create a review game.

Procedure: Put the students in groups of four and have each team come up with a review game that will be played at the end of class. There must be rules; it must involve all the students; and there must be one clear winner, whether it's an individual or a team.

Criteria: Rules_____
    Elaboration_____
    Original_____

Notes

Implementation _____

_____
_____
_____
_____
_____
_____
_____

Changes _____

_____
_____
_____
_____
_____
_____
_____

Results _____

_____
_____
_____
_____
_____
_____
_____

The Passport

Time: One Class Period
Materials: Various
Arrangement: Individual or Group

Scenario: Travel around the world at your desk.

Procedure: Your students should create their own passport with a few sheets of paper. It's like a little review book and they should write down several important facts about each country in your unit of study. They can receive a 'visa stamp' after completing a brief quiz about the country. Students should look up the information that is included in a real passport and add it to theirs.

Criteria: Content_____
　　　　　Factual_____
　　　　　Original_____
　　　　　Aesthetics_____

Notes

Implementation_____

_____
_____
_____
_____
_____
_____

Changes_____

_____
_____
_____
_____
_____
_____
_____
_____

Results_____

_____
_____
_____
_____
_____
_____
_____

Symbolic Map

Time: One Class Period
Materials: Various
Arrangement: Individual or Group

Scenario: Put some culture all over that map

Procedure: Students can create a map of a specific country or region that is relevant to the unit of study. After researching about the area's culture, the students can draw what they've learned on the map.

Example: Getting more specific… If a student were to create a map of Europe, instead of drawing the typical 'star' where the capital goes, the students could draw a symbol that truly represents the country. Italy = bottle of wine, France = Eiffel Tower, Ireland = shamrock

Criteria: Content_____
         Factual_____
         Original_____
         Aesthetics_____

Notes

Implementation _____

_____
_____
_____
_____
_____
_____

Changes _____

_____
_____
_____
_____
_____
_____
_____

Results _____

_____
_____
_____
_____
_____
_____

Foldable

Time: 20-30 Minutes
Materials: Various
Arrangement: Individual or Group

Scenario: Perfect way to review!

Procedure: There are too many types of foldables to explain here, but the basic foundation is simple enough. Students need to review material in order for it to make into their long term memory, but reviewing can be tedious, so why not make it a little more fun. One simple foldable is to cut a sheet of paper into a square and fold each point so that the point touches the center of the square. When it's closed, have the students write four questions on each of the points, with the answers on the inside. This can be manipulated and used in a variety of ways.

Criteria: Content_____
  Factual_____
  Original_____

Notes

Implementation_____

_____
_____
_____
_____
_____
_____

Changes_____

_____
_____
_____
_____
_____
_____

Results_____

_____
_____
_____
_____
_____
_____

Creative Journal

Time: All Year
Materials: Various
Arrangement: Individual

Scenario: Keeping a journal throughout the entire year filled with any of the activities in this book.

Procedure: At the beginning of the year, have your students bring a spiral notebook to use as their creative journal. It can be used as a nightly homework assignment, or worked into your daily lessons. I would usually have my students complete one exercise per lesson.

Criteria: Content_____
          Factual_____
          Original_____
          Aesthetics_____

Notes

Implementation _____

_____
_____
_____
_____
_____
_____

Changes _____

_____
_____
_____
_____
_____
_____
_____
_____

Results _____

_____
_____
_____
_____
_____
_____

Wear It!

Time: One Class Period
Materials: Various
Arrangement: Individual

Scenario: Be a model for any culture.

Procedure: Students should research a different country's clothing and put together an outfit to wear on a certain day at school. During class each student should come in front of the class and allow the other students to ask questions about what they're wearing.

Example: Lederhosen, kimono, ao dais, black garbed pilgrims, kilts, sari, ponchos, bombachas, galabiyah, or tunics

Criteria: Participation_____
            Factual_____
            Original_____

Notes

Implementation _____

_____
_____
_____
_____
_____

Changes _____

_____
_____
_____
_____
_____

Results _____

_____
_____
_____
_____
_____

Social Studies for the Competitive Mind

1. The Chain Game

Similar to the game show, this is a chain reaction game in which the students must say two-word phrases that relate to the course. The first letter of the first word must be the same as the previous student's first letter of the second word.

Notes

Changes_____
_____
_____
_____
_____
_____
_____

2. The Grand Prize Game

Set it up like Bozo the Clown. You will need plastic cups or containers spaced out and a ping pong ball to toss. After each successful toss, you must answer a review question to go on to the next shot. Have a prize to give, or be the funny mean teacher and give them nothing! HAHA

Notes

Changes_____
_____
_____
_____
_____
_____
_____

3. Pick-Up Sticks

Like the old game 'Pick-Up Sticks', have some Popsicle sticks labeled with states, countries, or any other concept. If you pick up Georgia, then you must say, 'Atlanta' and so on. The student with the most sticks at the end wins a prize.

Notes

Changes _____

_____
_____
_____
_____
_____
_____
_____

4. Hot Potato

Get something to pass and start some music. This is great for geography or chronological events. If the music stops before you can answer and pass it, you're out!

Notes

Changes_____
_____
_____
_____
_____
_____
_____
_____

5. Stump the Teacher

Hopefully you know what you're teaching! Have the class come up with review questions for you to answer. They will love trying to stump you. If you know 'everything', then throw a bone every now and again. This is great for learning capitals.

Notes

Changes_____
_____
_____
_____
_____
_____
_____
_____

6. Elimination

Classic review game. Just ask review questions before a test and whoever is incorrect is out. Make them sit on the floor to get a rise out of them.

Notes

Changes_____

_____
_____
_____
_____
_____
_____
_____

7. Bingo

Another great game for geography or presidents. You'll need to label cards appropriately and don't make it too easy. If you label it with the names of presidents, don't just say the names, but give facts about them.

Notes

Changes_____
_____
_____
_____
_____
_____
_____
_____

8. Hangman

Words or phrases about the lesson you're teaching. This is great on a rainy-day recess and the younger students will forget that it's learning...

Notes

Changes_____
_____
_____
_____
_____
_____
_____

9. Basketball

Get a Nerf hoop for the door and turn it into a review game. Always fun. Combine it with elimination and make it so you can get back in the game if you make a basket.

Notes

Changes_____
_____
_____
_____
_____
_____
_____

10. The Hunt

Hide clues or questions around your class or school that relate to your lesson. (Use old Easter eggs). Whoever gets the most wins (or answers the most).

Notes

Changes_____

_____
_____
_____
_____
_____
_____
_____

www.ingramcontent.com/pod-product-compliance
Lightning Source LLC
Chambersburg PA
CBHW060158050426
42446CB00013B/2886